LIVE STREAMING BASICS

EVERYTHING YOU NEED TO GET STARTED

SIMPLY EXPLAINED

MASSIMO COLOSO

To Neri & Righetto

CONTENTS

PREFACE

A few years ago, when I first got involved in live streaming, I wish I had had the opportunity to count on a manual like the one you now have in your hands. I would not have thought twice and would have raced to the bookstore to buy it. Having no mentor to whom I could refer to and guided only by my passion for this new and intriguing activity, every little technical doubt became a seemingly insurmountable obstacle: figuring out how to solve it forced me, at times, to spend whole days researching on English-language forums (I'm Italian) that, at least, I am lucky enough to understand well. I did not decide to write this book; it wrote itself. It happened because over time, I noticed that manuals

7

'simply explaining' the subject of streaming still do not exist and, if they do, I have not been lucky enough to come across them. There are, indeed, some manuals devoted to the world of TV and video shooting but, in my opinion, they are characterised by an overly technical exposition that on a few occasions, in all honesty, I have struggled to understand. Whilst it is true that such technicalities are probably useful to the student engaged in tackling a university exam, it is equally true that very little is of any use to multimedia enthusiasts and professionals entering the world of real broadcasting for the first time.

Personally, I wished to offer a contribution that would explain simply, not superficially, how to produce conscious and good quality streaming.

Happy reading!

STREAMING:
WHAT IT IS AND HOW IT WORKS

The word streaming defines the delivery method of any kind of multimedia content carried in real time from a broadcast source (server) to a receiving device (client) such as a TV, a PC, a laptop, or a smartphone. More simply, the multimedia file, which has already been previously stored on a remote server, is transmitted from that server a few seconds (data packets) at a time in order to be enjoyed on the device of the recipient user (client). This peculiar system of multimedia transmission differs from the classic element downloaded on the memory of a hard disk because of this method of delivery, which allows the immediate fruition of the content. The user can then start the playback of the audio/video content without having to wait for the full download of the file on their local storage media, which will not even affect its storage capacity (the file is not stored on the 'client' media, but only encoded and served by the browser).

If we downloaded a movie from a website or cloud storage, a copy of the entire file would be saved on our device's hard drive and the video would not be playable until the entire file was downloaded. When streamed, by contrast, the multimedia is delivered a few seconds at a time and the end user's browser takes on the workload of decoding it in real time, data packet by data packet, avoiding the long wait that would entail a full download of the file. It may be useful to think of the difference between a lake and a river: both contain water, but streaming can be compared to a river, where the water is never all in one place and reaches a specific point downstream a little at a time. Classic downloading can be compared to a lake which, occupying many cubic metres, is quite complex to transfer in a single act. When streaming audio and video data are divided into data packets each containing a small part of the file. Upon receiving this information, the client-side (end-user) media player will re-encode these data packets, consisting of sequences of numbers, into a browser-readable audio/video file.

It is important to remember that for the playback of particularly heavy digital files already present in the local memory, and for the reproduction of streaming media, the receiving device must have a hardware system agile enough to manage and process the amount of data received. In order to enable the enjoyment of streaming broadcasts, media files intended for this type of use are, in almost all cases, processed by degrading encoding (often imperceptible) and are characterised by a lower quality than media usable from classic hardware media, such as internal/external memories and DVDs.

Two transport protocols are most widely used for streaming transmissions, and they differ in reliability and transmission speed. These are TCP (Transmission Control Protocol) and UDP (User Datagram Protocol).

In the case of the TCP protocol, a dedicated connection is opened between the server and the client (end to end) which ensures that all packets are sent from point A to point B in full and sequential order. If a loss of data occurs, this protocol also reschedules the transmission of the lost packet, thus ensuring that the transmitted file is received in full (a reliable but slower system).

With the UDP protocol, no dedicated channel is defined for transmission, and data packets are neither transmitted sequentially nor retransmitted in the event of a data loss. Transmission is much lighter and faster but the risk of losing some information along the way increases.

In practical terms, the TCP protocol is used when there is a need to transfer from point A to point B the totality of the required information given that it turns out to be a secure protocol which guarantees the integrity of the delivery (almost all video-on-demand platforms such as Netflix or Amazon Prime and all security, military or medical communications use this protocol). The UDP protocol, on the other hand, is more widely used for streaming transmissions such as video conferences and online meetings because it is faster and if some data is lost (e.g., a frame of the video or a small audio particle) the end user is still able to understand the logic of what is happening to be able to proceed in the conversation. Thus, there is no strict requirement that the data sent, and the data received matches perfectly.

A brief note is useful to define the concept of 'buffer' (how many times have we dealt with it?). All media players, client-side, load a few seconds of 'information' in advance, a kind of data buffer that is used in case the flow of data is briefly interrupted. When this happens, the media player serves the end user the buffer containing the data that the client device loaded in advance (when the data stream was smooth) thus allowing the client to keep enjoying the media stream without noticing anything. Buffer loading can be particularly slow when the geographical distance between point A and point B (server and client) is large. If, to give an example, from Italy, I watch streaming content that is allocated to and transmitted from a server located in Australia, the data packets will have to travel thousands of miles to transfer between the two extremes. In cases like these, in relation to on-demand content platforms such as Netflix or Prime, so-called CDNs (Content Delivery Networks) step in.

Content Delivery Networks are nothing more than servers physically located in different parts of the world that contain exact copies of the same files in Singapore, as well as in Sydney, Amsterdam, or New York. In this way, a viewer from Italy will not have to refer to the original server in Australia but will instead be able to watch the same movie by interoperating a connection with a CDN located in Amsterdam, gaining in terms of lower latency and therefore enjoyability of multimedia content.

HISTORICAL BACKGROUND

If we were to ask a thousand inhabitants of planet earth about when, in their opinion, multimedia streaming was born, we can bet that from most respondents we would get an incorrect answer. Likely, they would answer that streaming applied to multimedia content is a recent invention, consequent to the implementation of the first Internet networks. Alas, the answer would be incorrect. Would you believe it if I told you that the first experiments, admittedly successful ones, of multimedia transmission technically definable as 'streaming' date back as far as the nineteenth century and more precisely to the late 1800s? That's right. In fact, it was back in 1881 when the

'Compagnie du Théâtrophone' allowed its subscribers to listen to opera and other theatrical performances on the bill live over the first rudimentary telephone lines. Théâtrophone was an active broadcasting system in Europe that allowed subscribers to listen to live performances over the telephone line. The first public demonstration of this new technology took place in Paris in 1881 and was technologically very advanced for its time, put on by Clément Ader at the 'International Electricity Exhibition.' Monsieur Ader set up eighty telephone transmitters in front of the stage, creating the first form of audio transmission that could be defined as stereo (binaural) and allowing listeners located in a room more than two miles away to hear artistic performances by means of headphones to be placed on their ears. Victor Hugo, who was present and was able to test this new technology for the first time, described his experience as *very pleasant*. To give an idea of the success this novelty achieved, suffice to say that only a few years later, in 1884, King Luís I of Portugal asked to be allowed to use Théâtrophone to listen to opera on days when he would not be able to physically reach the theatre. He was accommodated by the director of the Edison Gower Bell Company who was later awarded the 'Military Order of Christ' as an act of gratitude for services rendered.

In 1906, in the United States (however, the original patent dates back to 1897) a very special music streaming service was inaugurated: it was based on an instrument called a Telharmonium. Initially known as a Dynamophone, the Telharmonium weighed around two hundred tons and was an assortment of rotors, switchgear, and transformers; Essentially, a sort of present-day synthesizer. Partly due to the intervention of technicians-musicians present at the keyboard-console, it produced music 24 hours a day. Subscribers, by calling the switchboard, could ask to be connected to the telephone line that transmitted the sounds of the Telharmonium in order to receive live coverage of the amazing melodies that this instrument produced. Mark Twain, the famous American writer, who was an avid admirer of the Telharmonium, was heard saying, '*Every time I see or hear a new wonder like this, I feel like postponing my death.*'

The 'on-demand' evolution of a service like that offered by the Telharmonium was the technology served by the 'Telephone Music Service' from 1930. Here, the subscriber could request his or her favourite piece of music by talking directly to an operator who, in a specially set up room in Pittsburgh, would take about 20 seconds to locate, from among the thousands of records stored on the shelves, the right 78, 45 or 33 rpm record to put on the turntable platter to return the requested audio to the user via telephone cable.

But when can we say the age of streaming media as we 21st-century men and women understand it really began? In 1993, apparently. In fact, the anecdote that follows is officially recognized by several sources as the first real Internet streaming produced in recent times. On June 24th, 1993, the band 'Severe Tire Damage' was called to play at the Xerox PARC in Palo Alto, California, at an event where some engineers and researchers were presenting a new technology called 'Mbone'. This technology was useful for broadcasting multimedia content online. As a test of how this worked, the band's performance was broadcasted online to allow it to be viewed by the few users in the world who, at that given time, could enjoy a sufficient broadband connection. In an interview in March 2017, band member Russ Haines stated that to broadcast the concert, technicians used practically '*half the bandwidth globally available at that time.*' All this for multimedia content of only 152 × 76 pixels with a frame rate of 8/12 frames per second and audio quality comparable to, according to the band members themselves, a bad phone call. The die was cast, however. Since that time, thanks to the very rapid development of computer technology, the ever-increasing bandwidth implemented by providers and the decreasing costs of home subscriptions, the platforms distributing on-demand streaming content - on par with current ones such as YouTube, Amazon Prime and Netflix - have been able to enjoy an unstoppable and growing appreciation by users so much so that for decades they have been among the most visited websites in the world.

So far, we have dealt with some introductory aspects that could not be skipped for the purpose of providing both a complete and exhaustive overview and better understanding of the topics that we are going to discuss from here.

Therefore, the time has come to understand how to produce multimedia streaming.

CONTENT FOCUS

The moment we decide to assemble our own setup to stream content, a prior and thorough analysis of what we are going to convey online is necessary to really understand our needs are. Personally, I do not find it reasonable to spend ten thousand dollars on a professional video camera or video capture card if your intention is to broadcast a simple game session. Of course, if the budget allows, do so; the choice is obviously subjective. In most cases, however, those approaching streaming as novices have a limited budget and the need to carefully consider how to spend their money. So, whether you wish to stream your online gaming sessions, produce a video blog, or assemble a professional setup to be used for your company's communications, it is important that you pause for a moment to think carefully about what your primary needs are. Understanding what we really need is not only about economics but also about management. Imagine how complex it would be for a gamer to manage the direction of his show, simultaneously interacting with a sound mixer, video mixer, chat and lights while trying to hit an enemy hiding behind a tree at the top of the hill. The setup needed in this case will have to be easy-to-manage hardware that the gamer will be able to control with the movement of a finger. However, if the broadcast system you are going to implement can rely on one or more dedicated operators, then you will not only be able to achieve spectacular and higher quality live streams, but also minimize the real risk of incurring macroscopic errors.

The management aspect also includes the evaluation concerning the platforms that you intend to interest with your live broadcast. In fact, it is rarely possible to broadcast a quality signal simultaneously on two platforms - for example, on two different social networks - without relying on a cloud service to take on that responsibility for you. Because yes, it is a responsibility, if you want to get it right. It is true that technically broadcasting to multiple destinations is possible on your own, but that means doubling or tripling the need for upload bandwidth (good luck with that) and doubling or tripling the efforts of your encoding software/hardware which, you will realize by trying, will already be very busy by the time it has to deal with a single instance. To be fair, technology has changed in recent months; the latest video cards (the Nvidia 30 and 40 series, for example) have in fact received a driver update that increased their inherent encoding capability from three instances to five. This means that two or three simultaneous encodings to multiple destinations can now be tackled with greater peace of mind, provided you are operating on a balanced, stable and bottleneck-free hardware system. In short, it can be done, but I urge you to carefully consider using this solution, unless you're planning a setup to reach Mars and have an exclusive partnership with a network provider that can supply you with the appropriate upload facility.

How then do so many streamers broadcast simultaneously on both Twitch, Facebook, and YouTube? The answer is simple: they pay. There are numerous online services specifically dedicated to this function. Using these virtual platforms, you will be able to transmit a single signal to their servers which will process, multiply and forward your data to as many destinations as you wish. The problem with these kinds of portals is that they are not cheap. They start from a minimum annual cost of $150 up to $450 per year for the professional plan that you almost always need in order to enjoy all the available options.

In conclusion, a distribution service for your

live broadcast will allow you to multiply your broadcasting power, even if you are in the middle of the countryside with a meagre 4G signal. It's useful on numerous occasions, but it will be necessary to splash out.

THE BANDWIDTH

Well, no, we're not talking about live bands and musical performances. In our case, it is the upload and download data packets that are playing. Let's proceed and take a closer look at this fundamental aspect of live streaming.

So-called bandwidth is the ability of our network to receive or send data from or to an external server. Thus, available download bandwidth refers to the amount of Mbps (Megabits per second) your network system can transfer from an external location to your local location, while upload bandwidth, refers to the amount of Mbps you are able to transfer from your location to the external server. Now, if you are reading this book it is because you wish to start with A/V streaming (Audio/Video streaming), so I must give you some bad news right away: to transmit multimedia data to the outside world, you will need considerable and stable upload bandwidth. Too bad that such bandwidth, in almost all cases, may rely on network availability that turns out to be only a tenth of the bandwidth generally dedicated to downloading. This happens because most home and business users have the primary need to download data from the Internet rather than upload it. Ninety percent of the traffic that passes through network routers is traffic used to visit websites and receive information included in e-mails or featured in the tutorial you are about to watch online; this is all data that is downloaded, not uploaded. Infrastructures are designed and structured to favour download bandwidth rather than upload bandwidth, and this is something that we streamers get a lot of data packet spinning (that's a metaphor), since it significantly complicates our work. In fact, without adequate upload bandwidth, the broadcast is almost certainly doomed to fail. An additional technical value that is sometimes useful to consider when we are about to stream content is latency (ping). It is directly proportional to the distance between our workstation and the remote server to which we are broadcasting. A greater distance will result in greater latency and imply, at best, a larger buffer and a less satisfactory client-side (end user with frequent signal interruptions) user experience. However, it should be considered that you will rarely, at least in my direct experience, find yourself sending your A/V feed over sidereal distances; generally, the servers that run the most common streaming services are tactically located in all major geographic areas of the world to enable us 'to talk' to relatively close hubs. Therefore, unless you are asked to route your data specifically to a private server allocated in China, the latency issue needs to be evaluated, but remains something you don't need to worry too much about.

Last, but not least (indeed!), there is the Bitrate (measured in kbps, Kilobits per second) that you intend to assign to your encoder and thus to your transmission. The bitrate value represents the amount of audio/video data packets present in the signal you transmit. The higher the bitrate, the higher the quality of your stream; colours will be brighter and images sharper. Let me give an example; imagine you need to paint a wall red. With the first coat (so a limited amount of paint) you will get a faded result and smudged outlines. With the second coat, the result will be better, and with the third, you will get a sharp and bright result. In conclusion, the more data that makes up a frame of your video (the more paint on the wall), the better the result will be. It is a matter of quantity, data, and paint.

Depending on the upload bandwidth available to us, you will therefore need to make a prior assessment of the bitrate value to be used, since this value significantly changes, one way or the other, the amount of data your encoder processes and sends over the network. It can sometimes happen that a broadcast with a lower resolution (HD), but with a higher bitrate, is sharper than a broadcast with a higher resolution (Full HD), but with a lower bitrate. You then see that determining what resolution and bitrate to use for a stream is a matter of hardware, technical knowledge, and personal sensitivity. You will have to make the assessments yourself from time to time, taking into consideration the network performance of the facility in which you are operating. The amount of bandwidth we will need in order to produce a quality broadcast changes according to both the resolution at which we intend (or can, if bandwidth is limited) to transmit and according to the number of 'frames per second' (fps) you will need to set.

Generally, applying to both HD and Full HD resolution broadcasts, if we are streaming a conference or event where the speakers move relatively little and the scenery remains mostly unchanged, the useful frames per second will never be more than 30. Conversely, if we are covering a sporting event where the players are moving quickly from one side of the field to the other and the ball is moving just as fast, it will be necessary to stream at 60 fps to allow a smooth viewing of the game to those watching from home. So, to greatly simplify, if the scene is 'stationary,' you will set 30 fps, while if it is 'moving' fast the fps will rise to 60. Consider that each situation will then also have to be evaluated according to your personal experience and the robustness of the network. If you can count on an upload speed of 100 Mbps, (it is rare but sometimes possible) no one can stop you from broadcasting even a simple conference in 4K at 60 frames per second. A technical note that I have guiltily taken for granted: to test the quality of your network, there are applications such as Ookla Speed Test (you can find many of them on the app stores) that you can use either from your PC, if it is wired via Ethernet cable, or from your smartphone in case you are - but I really hope not - planning to broadcast using the wi-fi of your phone's hotspot.

The following are rough values for almost any situation in which you will find yourself operating. It is the only time in this publication, I promise, where I will bore you with two short pages of purely technical values that I report for completeness, considering they may come in handy in the future.

If after on-location testing you find that you have available upload bandwidth ranging from 2 Mbps to 5 Mbps, it is advisable to broadcast with a resolution of 720p (1280 x 720) at 30 frames per second with a maximum bitrate of 4000 kbps and a minimum of 1500 kbps. If you wish to send to the network the same resolution at 60 frames per second, the necessary bandwidth you will need rises to a range from 3 Mbps to 8 Mbps, whilst a bit rate between 2000 kbps and 6000 kbps will be suitable.

With an upload bandwidth ranging from 4 Mbps to 8 Mbps, it is recommended to broadcast with a resolution of 1080p (1920 x 1080) at 30 frames per second with a maximum bitrate of 6000 kbps and a minimum of 3000 kbps. In case you wish to deliver the same resolution at 60 fps, the required bandwidth rises to a range from 6 Mbps to 11 Mbps with a bit rate of between 4500 kbps and 9000 kbps.

If the upload bandwidth is between 8Mbps to 16Mbps, it will be possible to broadcast with a resolution of 1440p (2560 × 1440) at 30 frames per second with a maximum bitrate of 13000 kbps and a minimum of 6000 kbps. For streaming at 60 fps, the required bandwidth will have to be between 11 Mbps and 22 Mbps with a bit rate that can be set between 9000 kbps and 18000 kbps.

Broadcasting in 4K is a dream, indeed a utopia, however in some situations it may be possible. In this case, at 30 fps you will need an upload between 16 Mbps and 41 Mbps and a bit rate between 13000 and 34000 kbps. At 60 fps, the bandwidth needed will go up to between 26 Mbps and 60 Mbps, whilst the bitrate can be set between 20000 kbps and 51000 kbps.

Practical note: The first thing to do when a customer hires you for a live streaming, and I reiterate the first, will be to inquire what kind of network is located where the event will take place. It is by no means enough for them to reply, 'There is an Internet line' or 'We have fibre,' to be reassured. The venue may have fibre, but if the fibre is shared via Wi-Fi with all the speakers and spectators in attendance, sometimes thousands, you will end up with a slow upload that will be the antechamber of disaster. It is therefore necessary to understand exactly what the upload potential of the network is and ask the hall manager to contact the IT technician in order to have a line reserved exclusively for your live broadcast. Indeed, it is usually a good idea to get the technician's contact information and talk to him in person for a chance to explain in detail your needs and receive assurance about the work he will do to secure that service for you (it's his job, so insist it).

It is important to emphasise this, because it is technically not us who offer the mobile directing service who are responsible for the performance of the network present in the location. The only exception to this is if the client explicitly requested beforehand for us to implement ourselves in the room, via satellite or 'bonding' (we will see later what this is), the Internet line that we will need. In my own case, for example, there is a clear and visible clause at the drafting of the contract that refers to what, and whose, responsibility it is for the proper functioning of the network. The reason that we act in this way is quickly explained. The average customer takes for granted that for a live broadcast, the network issue is secondary. Unfortunately, instant live video from

Facebook and IGTV have promoted the idea that the bandwidth needed for a live broadcast is always available. That may be true, but what quality are we talking about? The customer therefore does not consider the problem related to network robustness, and it is a good idea to specify when defining the terms, that our service will rely on the (Inter)net already in place at the venue unless explicitly requested by the customer, which will eventually affect the final costs in no small way. This is theory. The practice is quite different, unfortunately.

Because, you see, there are two different aspects to this question: the technical one that we just discussed, and the practical one that I am going to explain. It is true that the responsibility for the operation of the network often does not fall on the mobile directing service (i.e., us) because it is the liability of the venue hosting the event, but the moment they fail to devote the necessary line to you and the transmission goes jerky or crashes for whole minutes (minutes of panic), who do you think the enraged customer will go to for an explanation? To us! And it won't be easy to explain to him that we did an impeccable job, and we are not responsible for the failure of the broadcast. In their eyes we 'were not capable' of implementing the stream. Rest assured; exactly this will happen!

For this reason, it is always in our interest to know what we will be facing in terms of bandwidth availability in order to put all precautions in place that will allow us to bring home a good job. There are two aspects to consider: the first is the ability to modulate the transmitted signal, in terms of resolution, fps and bitrate, according to the available bandwidth, whilst the second is related to testing: the sacrosanct tests. As far as I am concerned, in order to avoid any unforeseen events, I have travelled up to one hundred miles to carry out an on-location upload test in advance, usually a few weeks before the event. It is true, I incur costs that no one will reimburse me for, but what I get in return is customer satisfaction, the chance to work serenely and an increase in the reputation of my company. This is no small thing, I assure you. Serious and painstaking work always pays off, but you are certainly aware of this.

WIRED vs WIRELESS

We have now seen how good bandwidth is essential to achieve a quality transmission that makes our streaming enjoyable to the viewer. How to properly exploit this bandwidth, however, is another important chapter that certainly needs to be explored. Is it better to connect via Wi-Fi or through an Ethernet cable? Also, is it advisable to rely on a landline network or rather one's modem or mobile phone thanks to mobile data? Let's go step-by-step, starting by defining as simply as possible the different technologies available to us.

MODEM: A modem is a device that enables connection to the Internet through the telephone line using the infamous twisted pair, found in almost all human construction, or a SIM for mobile data.

ROUTER: A router is the device (often the same one that houses the modem, especially in home systems) that allows the distribution to multiple devices (via WLAN, radio, LAN, or cable) of the data that is received thanks to the modem.

The modem then connects to the Internet while the router distributes that connection, via cable or radio waves, to available devices.

LAN: An acronym for 'Local Area Network,' a LAN is a network of wired local (home, office) connections. Each device connected to a LAN will then have a physical cable connecting it to the Internet access point (modem-router).

WLAN: An acronym for 'Wireless Local Area Network' that is a local connection network made via radio waves. Therefore, it is not necessary for the different devices to be physically connected to the modem-router.

WI-FI: The acronym 'Wi-Fi' (unverified info, as there is no officialdom) would be derived from the first syllables of the words Wireless Fidelity just as audio 'Hi-Fi' is derived from High Fidelity. Wi-Fi is a set of proprietary technologies that, thanks to radio waves (via WLAN), allows connection to an Internet access point (modem-router) to different types of devices such as smartphones, PCs, or smart televisions.

ETHERNET: The term Ethernet defines a set of proprietary technologies useful for building LANs, hence 'wired.' The function is the same as Wi-Fi with the only difference being that Ethernet was born to be used through wired connections. Although in distinct ways, both fulfil the task of connecting and transferring data between different devices.

Now with these terms simply defined, it is necessary to understand the advantages and disadvantages of using these systems in the streaming environment. Even to the uninformed, the idea of connecting to a cable to start streaming should not be taken for granted. You cannot imagine how many professionals (the home gamers we forgive, eventually) insist on using the WLAN (Wi-Fi) on site to stream their well-paid broadcast. Such an attitude is technically and ethically an unforgivable levity. Your encoder's connection to the router must be wired, no argument there. Is the concept clear? W-I-R-E-D.

Of course, a few unique cases may occur (although as I write this, I can't think of any), but all your efforts must go in the direction of wiring the system to the router, even at the cost of laying an Ethernet cable (Cat6 at a minimum) for fifty yards or more. Specifically in streaming, there is no competition between the two technologies, and I go on to explain why I do not hesitate to characterise such a comparison as impractical.

Wi-Fi technology is insecure, slower, prone to interference of any kind, and decidedly unstable. It's insecure for two reasons: one, because radio waves travel through space and can be intercepted by any device located nearby and configured for that purpose. The second is because of the encryption that protects the transmission itself. It is like an eggshell, easily pierced and decoded with software that can be found effortlessly online, putting your communications highly at risk. A Wi-Fi connection is also slower than a wired one: an Ethernet cable of a given category can reach a data transfer rate of 10 Gbit/s (Gigabits per second) whilst the Wi-Fi speed (if we are lucky enough), can reach 700 to 800 Mbit/s (Megabits per second). An abysmal performance compared to Ethernet. The Wi-Fi connection is also prone to radio interference of any kind, from the TV to the microwave, rather than the microphone system implemented inside a conference room. In addition, Wi-Fi radio waves often need to overcome physical obstacles such as walls and doors. And that's not even considering the radio frequency your router uses to distribute the signal. It can easily become saturated since most home routers use the same radio channels. If you live in an apartment building, imagine how many routers can, at any given time, use the same frequency to convey the internet signal to the different connected devices, drastically slowing down your ability to send and receive data.

Whilst an Ethernet cable is virtually unassailable both from a security point of view (to intercept you, anyone with malicious intent would have to be physically connected to your network) and from the interference side, which are practically zeroed. Ethernet is a stable end-to-end communication with essentially no weaknesses, providing you use well-maintained, quality cables.

The elements we have considered so far in this chapter have been about connections and good practices to put in place when we are setting up our local system.

But the network, the real one, the one that serves us on a silver platter, the bandwidth we are going to exploit for our broadcast lies outside. It also travels on different but parallel tracks, either by cable or by radio waves, just like Wi-Fi and Ethernet. We are of course talking about network providers. Whilst it is true that locally, good practices guide us towards a forced choice, connecting to network providers will put us ahead of choices that may be different sometimes, at least based on my personal experience. Landline connections currently do not, apart from exceptional cases, appear to perform as well as mobile data connections, especially if the latter is handled consciously. In all the locations in which I have streamed, I have performed numerous tests of upload and download bandwidth capacity before the event. It regularly happens that the fixed line proves to be significantly slower than the mobile modem-router connection (large theatres or convention halls in metropolitan cities should be excluded from such personal statistics of mine, which are now perfectly equipped). I am not sure if this is purely due to geographic location, but rather I think it is because in 90% of the cases, if we combine conscious management of a SIM in a high-end modem-router with the opportunity to take advantage of a BTS (Base Transceiver Station) located nearby, we get much more upload bandwidth than the fixed lines available to us by most convention, hotel and corporate realities of our beautiful country.

What does it mean to consciously manage the mobile facility that relies on a modem-router equipped with an embedded SIM? A world opens, a world of modem-routers of a completely different quality than the ones that come with the various providers' dedicated subscription, and a world of external settings and antennas that you can deploy to connect the system to the nearest (or best performing) BTS.

But let us go, again, step-by-step.

BTS (Base Transceiver Stations) are the big antennas we see set up just about everywhere in the cities and countryside around us. They are the structures that network providers deploy on the ground to enable the distribution of the Internet signal they then sell to us mere mortals for home connection, if we use an internet dongle at home, or for our smartphones when we are on the move. It is those antennas that accomplish the magic of anytime, anywhere connection and allow us to not only broadcast, but to watch a film or read an email wherever we are. Knowing the BTS, how they work, and their location allows us streaming professionals to be able to count on a truly irreplaceable ally.

The internet provider's fixed line capacity remains always the same, but the use of a high-end mobile modem-router, and possibly the opportune pointing of some directional antennas properly connected to the modem allow us to utilise much more bandwidth than we might imagine. It is certainly true that, as in the case of Wi-Fi, radio waves have major drawbacks, but the abysmal difference in performance between the average landline system and the mobile option typically justifies the use of the infamous radio waves, at least for the connection to the provider. If I find myself in a location where I have upload bandwidth of 5/10 Mbit per second (thus barely enough for my transmission) whilst connected to the landline, it is clear that, at the very least, I will consider doing a test with the mobile modem-router which will almost certainly give me - not always, but in most cases - more upload bandwidth and will allow me to broadcast a consistent, quality stream. Considering that for a Full HD broadcast, an upload of 6 Mbit per second is sufficient I ask you a question: do you think it is easier for this bandwidth availability to fail, due to a signal drop or momentary line saturation, with a network that on average offers me 10 Mbit upload (landline), or with one that on average offers me 40 Mbit upload (mobile data)?

The answer is 'automatic,' as a close friend would say. Except in rare cases of BTS clogging (for example, if there is a stadium nearby with 40,000 spectators simultaneously surfing the Internet by connecting with their smartphones to the same BTS) my choice will fall on the mobile connection that, starting from an availability of 30 or 40 Mbit per second in upload, will hardly ever drop below 15/10 Mbit/s, assuring me anyway and always the bandwidth I need to send my live broadcast on the net. The most recent event I had the pleasure of running the broadcast for, a federation Italian water polo Cup live on Rai Sport (a national sports channel), was all accomplished with a single data connection and a quality mobile modem-router.

In Rai, the infamous 'Transit Office' (it really

exists and oversees sorting video signals) insisted on asking me for different solutions, but once the tests finished, they capitulated by surrendering to the evidence. At the end of the event, they complimented the quality of the signal, confirming that I made the right choice on that occasion.

A very important note: The mobile data modem-router I use is a CAT 19 MIMO 4X4 capable of aggregating three bands simultaneously. It also provides the ability, through a control panel, to choose which bands to use. Therefore, it goes without saying that once on site, it is first necessary to delve into and research which and where the best performing BTS is, thanks to various apps available on the app stores (Opensignal or Network Cell Info Line, just to name two examples). The modem-router I use is also connected to two external antennas, one omnidirectional and one directional, allocated on a tripod that reaches a height of 9 Feet. The directional antenna is occasionally millimetrically pointed toward the nearest (or best performing) BTS, and the network provider I rely on is the one that offers the best coverage and speed, in most cases. Choosing two antennas of different kinds helps, in case of a sudden decrease in bandwidth, to contain the damage. If the BTS to which the directional is connected to becomes saturated, there will always be the omnidirectional one ready to lend a hand and vice versa.

So, when I write about hardware-aware management to be used for mobile data, that is what I am referring to: the ability to implement a data delivering system that is unquestionably better performing and ten times more powerful than the classic cheap modem providers usually give us when a SIM is activated. At all costs, I don't want to sing a mantra in favour of mobile data, but the choice regarding how to implement the connection to the network provider must be evaluated for each individual case according to what you find in your hands once you arrive at the venue hosting the event. If the speed test with the landline gives a positive result, one equal or superior to what the test with mobile data returns, it should always be preferred.

CHOOSING THE CONFIGURATION

The combinations of hardware that can be imagined to design a streaming configuration are truly endless. Basically, there are three macro sections that make up a complete setup, and they are as follows: audio/video source acquisition, live source processing, and signal transmission. Put simply, they are cameras, media servers (PC or hardware switcher) and encoders. Since there are dozens of different companies producing cameras, cables, capture cards, switchers and encoders, it is often a matter of experience, or painstaking research, to make the right choice regarding which parts to buy and how to implement and optimise them for production. We will then have one or more cameras connected to a video mixer (hardware or software) that will process the incoming video signals and send the 'program' (master output) to the reference encoder, which may also be hardware or software, for broadcast.

I specify these things because, I confess, when I first started to get serious about streaming, being a novice, I had some difficulty understanding what I would need to build a reliable system that could also be called professional. I remember when the dealer explained to me that I would need an encoder, I gave him a distressed look because I didn't know what he was talking about. But that's why I'm here, and that's the reason for this brief compendium: to explain streaming in simple, clear concepts that will allow anyone to understand, at the very least, the basics of this exciting activity. The setup you are going to implement will be a direct result of what your real needs are, that's a given. Are you a gamer? Have you been asked to stream the Sunday services of your parish? Has your boss asked you to stream the next meeting with sales managers in the East? Are you a video maker looking to expand your creative offerings? Lo and behold, each of these situations will need a different setup that will, alas, force you to buy completely different equipment. Why do I regret to tell you this? Well, as you will realise once you've spent a few hours surfing online stores looking for the hardware that matches your needs, you will find that many of the parts that will make up your system will be expensive. Definitely expensive.

AUDIO/VIDEO SOURCES

It makes sense to think that what we call 'audio/video capture' might involve only the incoming video feeds from the cameras, but this is not the case. During a live broadcast, it almost always happens that you also must capture multiple inputs from different external computers hosting PowerPoint files, multimedia elements such as photos and videos, or to import into the live feed a Zoom meeting, or a webpage hosting a real-time survey that you or the company that commissioned the job want to show the audience. It is therefore not so obvious that the only input feeds you will receive will be those from the cameras, although this type of feed is most often the preponderant one.

Let us discuss what features a camera must have to be used functionally in our live broadcast.

The first essential element to consider when purchasing a video camera for streaming is that it can produce a clean HDMI feed. What you need is a camera that allows the transmission of a video signal through the HDMI output to be completely cleared from any overlay elements. This is a detail that is not obvious at all: there are mid-to high-end cameras where this function is not enabled, and it is not even possible to enable it since they're not intended to be streaming cameras. In case you haven't figured out what clean HDMI feed is, I will explain it now. When you turn on the camera in the display you will always see all the information about the camera settings superimposed on the image you are framing. So, the camera will display, for example, the aperture value, the ISO value, the battery charge status, and a lot of other information that just as it does not appear in the recordings you should make sure never appear in the video feed you are about to send to the switcher through the HDMI output either. Otherwise, you would find yourself having purchased a video camera that is good for recording your children's birthday, but completely unusable in a streaming environment. So, remember that the clean HDMI function, or more professionally 'clean feed,' is really a must have.

There are several types of cameras available on the market. Let us define what features each category has so you can make as thoughtful a choice as possible. Let's start at the low end, the very low end.

WEBCAM: The simplest tool available to anyone who owns a computer is the webcam. You can use either a built-in webcam or an external one by connecting it via USB. The latter generally provides higher image quality and more options from a configuration standpoint. There are external webcams of very good quality, but I would never recommend them for streaming use given the basicness of these mediums. It is not possible to zoom (sometimes a very bad digital zoom is available) and you also cannot place them too far away from your control desk since the USB cables already degrade the signal after a few feet. In low light conditions they also become unusable. I included them in the list only because they do, in fact, exist.

SMARTPHONES: The build quality of mid- to high-end smartphones nowadays can produce Full HD video footage that, in good lighting conditions, rivals mid-range cameras. Just think of the video quality that a state-of-the-art iPhone can produce, and you quickly realize why entire feature films have been overtaken with this tool. Not only iPhones, but also Android smartphones of different brands can deliver unquestionable video quality. The objective limitation of such devices is that as soon as the light goes out, the quality immediately suffers due to the small size of the image sensors. Another disadvantage of smartphones in streaming is that the manner used to connect them to the video switcher is often Wi-Fi, which brings with it all the limitations that we have elaborated on before (latency and dropped frames).

ACTION CAMS: These are not a first choice for a live streaming setup given their reduced potential (small sensor, limited manual settings). Classic action cams can, however, prove very useful for close-up shots thanks to their wide-angle lens. In the case of a musical performance, it is possible to place them at the drummer's feet, to film the bass drum, or on the neck of the guitarist's instrument for very curious and impactful shots. Beware, however, that if used via wi-fi (as would be mandatory if placed on the guitar neck) the latency produced by these small cameras would make them basically unusable for a live broadcast due to the lack of synchronicity with respect to wired cameras. However, if you manage to bring the video feed from the action cam up to your switcher via cable through the micro-HDMI output, the footage may come in handy for your live production.

POINT AND SHOOT CAMERAS: Point and Shoot cameras are small cameras with a video recording function that produces good quality video that can certainly be used for valuable home streaming. Equipped with a micro-HDMI output, they can be an interesting choice both for their portability (they fit in your pocket) and for the quality of their video output (often 4K), especially if they are recent models. Also known as 'holiday cameras,' they're easy to use and get good quality images. You just need, as the name reminds you, to frame and shoot. They are rather expensive, and I personally believe that in the case of live streaming, for the same price, it is probably advisable to direct our attention toward camcorders, even entry level ones, which still offer features more useful to our cause.

MID-ENTRY LEVEL (CONSUMER) VIDEOCAMERAS: Probably the most widely used by streamers around the world, consumer camcorders come in many models with similar functionality. The discriminating factors when it comes to these video cameras are the quality of the construction materials, the size of the sensor (which can vary considerably between mid- to low-end and mid- to high-end models), the cost (from $300 to over $2000), and some technical features such as the option to connect an external microphone, or the power of the internal processor. Natively they are capable of handling intense workloads, but there is still no way to change the lens, which will therefore always remain the original one.

DSLR CAMERAS: With DSLR (Digital Single Lens Reflex) cameras, we enter a professional world made of excellent quality sensors that can work even in low light. The latter feature is particularly useful if we need to live stream from locations with artificial light such as convention halls or places of worship. These are classic mid-range photo cameras that in recent years have eroded an increasing share of the market to the mid-entry level video camera segment, given their excellent video quality and the advantage of being able to change lenses if necessary. It is possible to use them in both automatic and manual modes, and they always have a microphone input. A great number of filmmakers currently prefer to buy a DSLR camera with advanced video functions rather than a proper camcorder. However, there are some 'cons' that must be stated regarding certain rather important aspects, such as the eventuality that (for certain models only) they overheat after a few hours of use, or a system lockout that, in recording mode, stops them by default after a predetermined amount of time (usually 20 to 30 minutes). This lockout setting was provided by the manufacturers because on fiscal matters DSLR cameras are photo cameras and not video cameras, resulting in different import and taxation costs. In our case, however, it is possible to circumvent this lockout, because in the event of streaming use, the camera could be 'on' but not recording, so we can keep it operational for as long as necessary without the fear of experiencing preset lockouts. For long-lasting events, it is a case of providing yourself with a dummy battery (power cord that simulates the battery itself) so that you can connect it to the power supply and not be forced to deal with the battery life limit and its replacement.

PROFESSIONAL CAMERAS: These kinds of cameras are high-end and obviously have every function for broadcast use such as XLR microphone input, lens interchangeability, professional SDI video outputs (of higher quality and reliability than the classic HDMI), dual slots for both memory cards and batteries, and many other pluses that we won't discuss now, because if you are a beginner, they're likely not of interest to you at the moment. These cameras cost many thousands of dollars and are generally used by professional services working for established entities such as television broadcasters and multinational media corporations. While it is true that they are beyond the reach of most small-to medium-sized directing services, it is also true that it's still possible to rent them at a more than reasonable cost, should a specific need arise.

PTZ CAMERAS: I'm devoting a separate paragraph to this type of camera, which, while not a market novelty, has undergone a radical technical and functional transformation in recent years. This has led them to evolve from simple video surveillance cameras to the primary choice made by those involved in live streaming. PTZs (pan/tilt/zoom) are small cameras that have the peculiarity of being able to move their lens automatically on two or three axes, depending on the model. Since these are therefore dedicated means for a user base of industry specialists, whether security or video communication professionals, this hardware has a completely different use from traditional cameras. The first feature that differentiates them from classic cameras is their non-portability. It is always possible to move them from one location to another, but it is never advisable to use them by hand unless you want a disastrous result. They were not designed for this purpose, nor do they have a handle that allows for consistent handling during a live show. It is necessary to fix them (literally) to the wall or place them on top of a tripod or other stable support base. The control of these cameras is only possible from a classic internet browser through a management panel via IP, and every parameter related to the settings will be configurable only from the web interface and never directly from the camera itself, except for some basic parameters.

Why then are PTZs chosen as the primary cameras by many corporate, association, and religious entities given the less intuitive handling? Because of their versatility. They have numerous useful functions, one of them being the possibility of automated framing. In fact, the operator assigned to the director will be able to manage both the type of framing and the depth of zoom (but also many other parameters) from a local network, or via the Internet, whilst remaining seated at his or her control station which can be located, in extreme cases, even thousands of miles away. Therefore, there is no need for a cameraman, causing both savings in costs and human resources. There is also the option of programming the shots that the PTZ will take in advance. Once preset, these shots can be recalled thanks to an input that tells the camera which zoom to be applied and the right movement on the three axes. One input, one shot, another input, a different shot. In the case of situations when the points to be framed are always the same, such as the altar or pulpit of a church, this type of functionality proves useful to camera operators. There are also applications that allow the camera to recognise the movements of the speaker on the stage of a congress, totally automating the movements of the lens that will be able to follow him/her on the stage autonomously.

A very helpful and significant feature!

CAPTURE CARDS AND CONNECTIONS

No video signal would be possible to display in our control room if between the camera and the computer, assuming you had opted for a software rather than hardware directing solution, the infamous capture card did not come between. Such cards are electronic devices capable of acquiring a camera video feed by encoding it for proper reading by the directing device, which in this case will be your PC. Hundreds of models are available online from 15 euros and up. Each capture card on the market has different characteristics and different reputation: it is therefore important to understand well which one may be the right one for you. For my part, I can relate an anecdote from some time ago, when a client preferred the video quality I obtained by using a $20 Chinese capture card rather than the one produced by a much more emblazoned brand costing $280. And what's more, he was right! It's like the never-ending challenge between PC and Mac ultras, no one ever comes to an objective conclusion and at the end of the day the only solution is the one that perfectly dresses our needs. So, buy, test, choose.

Regarding the audio/video data transfer in 90% of non-strictly professional setups it is implemented through a HDMI cable that, linked to the HDMI output of the camera, carries the video signal (the clean feed we have already talked about) up to the capture card connected to the PC. Once the camera is connected to the capture card (and the card to the PC) the preview of what you are framing will be available in real time on the directing software. Summarising the distribution chain discussed so far, we will have the following structure: camera -

HDMI cable - capture card – PC.

In non-professional video cameras, a clean feed output solution via mini or micro-HDMI socket is almost always available. You will therefore need to purchase and use a cable that has a micro (TYPE D) or mini (TYPE C) HDMI connector at one end and the larger classic HDMI (TYPE A) connector at the other end. In the professional field, on high-end camcorders, the HDMI (High-Definition Multimedia Interface) video output socket is replaced or combined with the SDI (Serial Digital Interface) one. The latter guarantees a faster and better-quality data transfer, capable of reaching, without degrading the video feed, much greater distances than with an HDMI cable. The SDI socket also has the benefit of so-called BNC (Bayonet Neill-Concelman) connectors, which have the peculiarity that they can be secured to the device to which they are connected by means of a locking system. There would therefore be no risk of disconnection if your colleague, while walking, were to trip over the cable (bet on it?).

It is for these reasons that SDI cables are always favoured by professionals over the less secure HDMI cables, which instead find their natural use in connecting contiguous elements (TV and Xbox for example). Even when evaluating the type of connection useful to our cause, the choice is often subjective (only sometimes mandatory). Experience has taught me that it is certainly possible to connect two or more cameras via HDMI, even if placed 100 feet away from the director's control room, providing the cable used is of very good quality fibre optic.

A recent innovation in the landscape of connections that can be implemented between a video source and a control room is the so-called NDI (Network Device Interface). Developed by NewTek, NDI is a versatile and revolutionary professional audio/video sharing protocol over IP. It thus allows all devices connected to the same network to bidirectionally share multiple audio/video data streams, via single Ethernet cable, without necessarily relying on the use of HDMI, SDI cables or capture cards such as those I have just outlined. In terms of video quality and resources committed, the type of data compression (codec) used by NDI technology is probably among the highest performing currently available in the multimedia landscape. NDI is a useful technology in several scenarios and is often used to screen share external PCs or notebooks with the director's desk. Should it be necessary to import the video feed of an ongoing Zoom meeting, it will be possible to do so via Ethernet cable by connecting the two PCs, the director's PC and the PC hosting the meeting, thanks to a basic 1gbps router. Many manufacturers are also implementing NDI communication on next generation video cameras, sensing the incredible potential of this kind of data transport system (in some respects still immature), which, I hazard a prediction, in the very close future could replace any other multimedia communication technology between even geographically distant systems.

In cases where it is not possible to lay a cable between the camera and the main director's switcher (due to long distance or structural impediments such as walls or bleachers in a stadium), it is possible to use audio/video transmitters and receivers that allow a radio bridge to be established between the two ends of the system. They work exactly as you imagine: the transmitter connected to the camera sends A/V data to the receiver connected to the control room using radio waves. If the radio link is what you need, it is essential to purchase proven systems that whilst they do have significant costs, on the other hand guarantee signal stability and extremely low latency that facilitates synchronisation with wired cameras, if any.

A last option for receiving an audio/video signal concerns connections "in the field." Have you ever wondered, when on the Tv news you see the field reporter operating from a remote location, how can he forward his video feed to the TV station since the excellent video quality certainly does not reach the control room through a smartphone's data connection? Well, what we don't see is the cameraman who is wearing a backpack (a classic backpack like the ones to carry our schoolbooks in) which contains high-tech equipment. Inside his backpack we will find an encoder (the 'star' of the last stage of a streaming system, which we will explore in a moment) which, thanks to some linked USB modem dongles, (each equipped with a SIM from different providers) encodes and sends the audio/video feed from the camera to the main studio in real time, or with relatively low latency. The backpack contains a long-life battery that powers the encoder, USB dongles, and the cables needed to make the system work properly. The reason for having several USB dongles is that the greater the bandwidth availability, the higher the bitrate, the better the quality of the broadcast. If it ever happens that one of these network providers falls victim to a sudden drop in bandwidth, the others will still be available, which, by referring to different networks, will be able to make up for the drop in signal. Beware, however: it is not enough to connect several USB dongles to the encoder to add up their bandwidth. An advanced technology implementation is also required (available on some encoders only), which enables so-called "bonding," whereby it is possible to combine the bandwidth provided by different mobile data providers to obtain a single wide, powerful and reliable signal. Cellular network bonding (bonding) combines several 3G/4G/5G modems (and, if available, also Wi-Fi and Ethernet) into a single, very robust Internet connection that allows for optimal signal transmission to the control room. The combination of different network providers allows the operator to 'unpack' and distribute the audio/video data stream over multiple connections. Data packets are then coherently reassembled and served live by the main directing studio thanks to dedicated applications specifically designed to fulfil this purpose. To achieve the magic of bonding it is necessary to sign up for a subscription meaning that we'll have access to everything we need for the deployment of this advanced transmission system: thus, the backpack with the hardware, and the software that will encode the video feed coming from camera that will then be delivered due to the different networks linked to the encoder by USB dongles.

CONTROL ROOM

We have so far considered the first stage of a television production comprised of all the elements needed to receive and broadcast any kind of video footage: video cameras, cables, and capture cards.

The heart of a multimedia production, however, is the control room, which includes every hardware and software component that allows the real-time mixing of incoming video feeds which will then be blended into a finalized visual layout (called 'program') to be served to viewers. Without the control room, it would not be possible to switch between shots, add overlay titles and subtitles, or broadcast multimedia elements such as promotional videos, still shots, or any kind of vector elements (graphics, animations, etc).

Until just over a decade ago, the control room has always been hardware only: a physical machine then, to which multiple cameras were connected by cable, which were then mixed in real time by the operator who, by pressing buttons on the mixing console (video mixer), produced TV magic. It should be emphasised that hardware video switchers still today have by no means disappeared from production and are routinely used in almost all professional broadcast configurations. Their size, however, has fortunately been reduced considerably, and thanks to technological progress it is now easy to carry them inside a briefcase for comfortable transport. The general trend, however, is moving in a different direction, especially in the streaming environment. As has been the case in most human situations, the rise of the digital age has completely disrupted the television industry as well by producing new systems based on binary computation, hence the use of computers. At the present time, particularly regarding mixing video feeds and composing them for broadcast, digital management software has taken over in almost all directing systems; indeed, it has itself become the directing system. All incoming video signals are then captured by a high-performance workstation (PC) and managed on the same machine through a conventional monitor and dedicated directing software. We are therefore talking about a personal computer that does...everything! It captures video feeds, processes them and, eventually, encodes the master program for broadcast. In the streaming field this has produced a truly remarkable advantage by allowing portability of very complex and expensive configurations that in times past would have required a large van, if not a truck, to transport.

HARDWARE VIDEO MIXERS: even if, as

we have seen, hardware video controllers (i.e., mixers dedicated purely to mixing video feeds) are slowly going to be replaced by 'all-in-one' systems based on computers and software applications, such physical consoles still offer undisputed advantages and for this reason are preferred, in many situations, to the certainly more agile and inexpensive PC-based systems. Particularly in high-level productions (I'm referring to televisions and broadcast companies tout court) the hardware video mixer is still the undisputed king of the whole multimedia production chain, either because technicians prefer to have physical buttons to push rather than a mouse to move on a screen or because, objectively, a hardware video mixer is born to be and do only the video mixer and is designed with specifications totally dedicated to its master function, thus characterising it with a practically guaranteed reliability. A physical video mixing console is therefore more reliable in all its functions and has the advantage of being natively equipped with all the required inputs and outputs, such as

HDMI and SDI, which in a different setup would have to be implemented through dedicated capture cards. Since these are means reserved for a relatively small number of professionals, they are also virtually immune to any kind of malware attack. Security, therefore, is their main characteristic: both from the point of view of design and reliability and from the point of view of imperviousness to any system incompatibility or virus.

The absolute most popular video mixing hardware devices in streaming, and I emphasize in streaming, are those of the ATEM series produced by Blackmagicdesign, an Australian company founded by Grant Petty in 2002 that assembles systems for audio/video acquisition in the broadcast field and can count on a very wide range of video mixers that have costs ranging from 300$ to 10,000$. For the benefit of small and medium-sized productions, especially from 2019 onward, good hardware video mixers, have become available on the market at low costs. Being able to handle up to 4 video sources, they appear to be an excellent alternative for any medium-sized sports or congress event.

SOFTWARE MIXER VIDEO: Computers are a kind of wonderful magic machine with which you can perform hundreds of different tasks thanks to dedicated applications often available online even for free. Some of these applications, as you can well imagine, have the sole purpose of managing a live event. Such applications, in terms of functions available, allow a much more advanced live streaming management than any hardware video mixer since, as we have already seen, the latter is born with a single function and dies (hopefully not during a live event!) performing always the same function: mixing different video feeds in real time. A personal computer for streaming use, on the other hand, can rely on its computing power to perform many concurrently tasks: it allows us to mix incoming video feeds, elaborate them with subtitling and graphics, and broadcast the master program to the destinations of our interest, thus avoiding the need for an external encoder.

One PC, in short, solves a lot of problems.

Or does it?

Well, the thinking gets interesting...

Whilst it is true that the management of direction during a live broadcast is really simplified for us if produced with a PC, the problem that occurs arises on two points that with a physical direction instead remain undisputed: safety and reliability.

A computer was not born to take care of a video direction any more than to manage an Excel spreadsheet: it is the applications developed for that purpose that allow us to use it for either purpose. Since, therefore, it is the applications themselves that must be programmed correctly to work in compatibility with the PC. Considering the undeniable reality that each PC is assembled with different components, the reliability and operability of a non-dedicated system become, more often than we would like, a weak point to be evaluated with extreme caution; especially when using software that requires a lot of resources, as in the case of managing multiple video and audio feeds.

Imagine a live broadcast performed completely from a PC and imagine if it suddenly crashes, as sometimes it happens. You would suddenly find yourself with no more incoming video feeds, without the ability to process anything, with no video stream out, and no option whatsoever to continue your broadcast until a complete system reboot is provided. I don't think this is a pleasant scenario especially if you are doing a well-paid job and see weeks of painstaking preparation, done together with the client, fade away because of some hardware/software incompatibility flaw or because of a PC driver that randomly chooses to stop working (it happens, eehh if it happens..) Now, whilst it is true that it is possible for the situation I have just described to occur, it is equally true that a very good rate of broadcasts based on computer architectures run smoothly without any problems whatsoever. A question is in order, however:

do you really feel like basing your live show on something so precarious? It depends: if a system crash interrupts a game on Twitch well, whatever, you reboot and restart. If the system crash prevents the transmission of the finals of an international volleyball tournament broadcast live on the first French Tv network well, there, the matter becomes a tad more delicate. This is why the famous three rules of streaming, again, must be strictly applied 'Test, test and test'. The method I personally use when I decide a 'software based' live (rarely) is to simulate in every way the live broadcast, as I anticipate it will unfold in terms of resources committed and expected duration. I perform, in a nutshell, a stress test in the studio which will reveal to me whether there are unforeseen critical issues on the horizon that need to be resolved.

Also, there is the question of which hardware configuration the PC you are about to use to run your live streaming should have. It certainly cannot be a Chromebook, just to name the most unlikely example (because it is unlikely, isn't it!!??).

The minimum requirements then, and I emphasise minimums, for a PC or notebook whose purpose should be to run a virtual directorate should include an Asus Z390 motherboard, an Intel i7, i5 or AMD Ryzen 4000 series processor, an NVIDIA GeForce GTX 1650 video card, 16 GB of RAM and solid-state disks (SSDs) for installing software and managing some features such as replay (moviola). Online you will find dozens of different configurations and recommendations regarding how to assemble a streaming PC. The in-depth therefore, as I am neither a computer scientist nor is this a specific text but only an introduction to the broadcast world, I leave it to your in-depth research.

There are several apps that you can use to perform a live streaming, but the most widely used by far, covering 90 percent of streaming systems, are vMix and OBS Studio (Open Broadcaster Software). vMix is a paid professional application, developed by the Australian software house StudioCoast Pty Ltd, which makes its completeness its strong point. It runs on the Windows operating system only, which is, much to the chagrin of Mac lovers, the favourite and most used system by professional productions worldwide. Every single aspect involved in directing a TV production can be tackled with this application without any fears whatsoever: mixing video inputs, composing them in a TV visual context, broadcasting multimedia of all kinds, titling and subtitling, recording content, and finally streaming them even to three different concurrent destinations (provided there is enough upload bandwidth of course). It is software updated with great regularity by its developers, and whatever new features need to be rolled out to keep up with rapid digital progress are planned on a tight schedule. vMix is an extremely stable software when used on well-designed computers, and lots of tutorials are available online to help moderate the effort required to overcome a learning curve that has some difficulties. There are several versions of the software that range from a cost of 60$ for the basic one, which is unlikely to be enough, and reach, going through several steps that gradually add features, to 1200$ for the professional version.

OBS Studio is open source live-streaming software that is totally free and available for multiple platforms including macOS, Windows and Linux. Developed and constantly updated by a community of active and passionate coders, it boasts numerous features, including typically professional ones, and benefits from an intuitive user interface that allows easy understanding of its main functions. The fact that it is free and not officially distributed by a software house should not be misleading: with OBS Studio it is possible to produce a show just as much as it is possible to do so with the more advanced vMix; what changes is the number of options and functions available for managing and customizing the broadcast, which certainly cannot be compared to the options offered by its paid big brother.

Regarding which of the many available applications you should choose to start your streaming business, the most reasonable advice I can give you is to start with OBS, which is free and functional, and later, in case you need to level up, consider buying a version of vMix or possibly even Wirecast, which, of all the paid alternatives, appears to be the one that best can compete with the King of streaming software, His Highness vMix.

Interesting note: as I was writing this paragraph on vMix, I wondered what exactly the acronym that represents it, vMix, meant. Is its meaning Video Mixer, Vision Mixer, or something else? I thought of asking on the various social communities to see if anyone knew the real meaning of this acronym and the answers between the serious and the facetious were: Violent Myxomatosis, Velocipedes mystic interior xaviers, 5Mix, Vision Mixer, Video mixer.

To make a long story short, no one among the professionals who are on the dedicated online groups knew what the acronym meant, despite them all mentioning it daily. So, I thought I would ask directly to... vMix! The response from the kind support service was as follows: 'Hi Massimo, Thanks for your email. The vMix name is not an acronym and the "v" has no "official" meaning but rather can allude to any or all the following: 'Video / Vision / Visual / Virtual / Variable / Versatile / Veritable / Viable / Value'.

Arcane solved!

THE ENCODER

Whilst writing this text I have mentioned the infamous encoder on several occasions, without ever explaining what exactly it is.
I could have briefly mentioned its function in the preceding paragraphs, but the encoder is such an important part of the streaming production process that I chose to postpone any technical explanations until now to devote all the required attention to it.

If we were to play a little game and metaphorically associate the human body with a broadcast production, we could certainly define the cameras and the different video inputs as the eyes of a production, the director's desk as its heart and the encoder as... the legs! Everything obviously linked by the nervous system (the wiring) that can very well represent the different connections between the three sections (acquisition, mixing, encoding). So, why do I define the encoder as the 'legs' of a production?Because without the encoder, there would be no broadcast. In fact, the primary function of the encoder is to convert the video signal generated by the cameras, which is complex and heavy, into a lighter digital signal that can be easily streamed over the congested networks of the World Wide Web. Despite the increasing popularity of streaming technology, cameras are still not produced to broadcast but to record. The files we get when recording our video footage on a digital medium, such as a classic SD card, are so-called RAW files. These are heavy files that include extensive information in every respect: colour depth, high quality audio, high bitrate, all specifications that define an uncompromising image quality. Instead, when we must serve large amounts of data to thousands of devices across the planet, it becomes necessary to encode this data in a lighter (and objectively lower quality) format to allow the data packets to be transferred to their destination as quickly and fully as possible. The day is probably not far off when we could stream RAW files thanks to incredibly fast and technologically advanced quantum internet networks, but that moment has not yet arrived, or at least has not arrived in our homes. This is why the encoder is essential. To transform/encode a large amount of data into a format that can be digested by existing networks. How it is possible to reduce the size of a file is easy to understand with a practical example: if we are streaming a conference where there is a speaker on stage who is entertaining the audience, it is quite likely that the background, i.e., the wall behind the speaker, is always the same, still, unchangeable. The encoder can read this situation and instead of also continuously sending all the information related to the background, which always remains the same, it only processes the 'zones' of the image that include who is moving on stage, allowing a truly remarkable saving in terms of the amount of data packets sent. Similarly, the encoder limits the bitrate compared to the original footage. Due to various high-performance encoding protocols (codecs), these operations are almost invisible to the human eye. Give it a try: if you are in your living room watching a TV show from your sofa, which is surely a few metres away, try getting up and moving very close to the screen: you will immediately realise that what from a distance appears as a perfectly sharp image will clearly reveal itself as a visual event characterised by small squares that no, they are not the pixels of your TV set, but they are a blatant demonstration of the degrading encoding operation that the television networks also carry out. If you were able to view the same images in the original format these small squares in your TV would simply not exist or would be present in a very limited amount. The encoder then encodes the original images, degrading them, but allowing us to enjoy the multimedia content with a relatively short latency that usually, in the case of streaming, travels roughly around 20 to 30 seconds. As in the case of the direction, the encoding process of the raw video file can be based on a software application or on a hardware device. In the case of a physical encoder, i.e., hardware, we will have a small device connected via HDMI or SDI to the master output of the control room (the so-called 'program', i.e. the processed and finished audio/video signal that we wish to serve to the public) which will encode the live footage and then broadcast it to the preset RTMP or SRT address. When we use a software encoder, on the other hand, our programme does not have to physically leave the machine we are working on, but can be processed by the same software we are using for directing, for example vMix or OBS. An ever-present function within this type of application is in fact specifically that of encoding. The discriminating factor between the use of a software encoder and a hardware one is almost never substantial, both solutions produce a very similar result, given the same set parameters. The advantage of using an external device, however, lies in being able to rely on a piece of hardware (it's always the same old story) dedicated only to the specific function for which it was designed, minimising the risks arising from the fatigue of the CPU (processor) and GPU (video card) of the PC, which are already stressed by the other demanding directing functions (acquisition and source management).

The choice of professionals should always go in the direction of outsourcing each specific function to dedicated devices, maximising all the various stages of direction and minimising the risks due to the possible sudden failure of a PC, which appear real if it must deal with the entire production cycle: mixing, recording and encoding. The downside of using external encoding hardware, however, is the price which hardly ever falls below 400$ for a basic model. An expense that certainly makes a big difference since a software encoder works just as well, is free of charge and is almost always already included in the mixing software.

PLATFORM CHOICE

Live streaming activities by gamers, companies, and association entities have been growing exponentially for several years now. The coronavirus pandemic has increased everyone's need to communicate online with family members, followers or customers precisely because of the restrictive impositions that have resulted in the impossibility of physically moving from one geographic location to another. The digital market, as is often the case, reacted quickly to meet society's new communication needs. Just think of the Zoom meeting platform, which from a virtually unknown reality has seen a 413 percent increase in its turnover in the last year and a half: mind-boggling numbers. As the manager of a business that makes multi-camera directing its core business, I can confirm that we have had several occasions to cooperate with companies, relatively large ones, which on the occurrence of online meetings with salespeople or clients from Western and Eastern markets, who did not have the opportunity to move from their working headquarters, have mandated us to produce virtual broadcasts that transcend the classic Zoom video call, in order to convey a high-level corporate image: So with the use of a green screen, set lights, skilled technicians and whatever else would be useful on each different occasion. Every company, alas, uses different platforms for its internal communications: GoToMeeting, Zoom, Cisco's Webex and others. I must admit that it was a true odyssey, especially in the early days, to understand from time to time the detailed functioning of each of those platforms which, whilst possessing similar features, certainly offer very different interfaces. As I have already pointed out in writing about setup design, the platform choice on which to broadcast must also be tied to what you foresee your target audience to be. All major social networks have now rolled out advanced live broadcasting systems: TikTok, Facebook, Instagram, Twitter, Twitch, Linkedin, Vimeo. The features offered by each of these platforms differ in some respects: some allow for monetization of the broadcasted content, some provide more detailed analytics, some the option of using a live chat to engage users, and some provide more security and privacy by offering the chance to access the live show with confidential login credentials only. It is therefore needed to be able to analyse properly what the specificities of the offer we are going to provide live are: a gamer will broadcast on Twitch, a company that wants to keep its customers and collaborators up to date will more reasonably broadcast on LinkedIn, a business that wishes to promote its activity aimed at a young or very young audience will rely on live broadcasts on what is currently their social of choice, Tik Tok. A major drawback, however, of all the platforms mentioned so far is that under no circumstances will they be able to offer you quick assistance when you need it. For this reason, best practices for professional live streaming of virtual meetings and events of all kinds should involve the use of private servers knowingly set up by specialised companies. They will not only be able to set up the machines following exactly the guidelines that we professionals will require from time to time, but they will also be able to intervene promptly in case any unforeseen event arises.

It is the same gap that arises between a large retailer and a craftsman: two similar worlds but considerably 'far apart' if we look at the quality of the services offered.

SET-UP HYPOTHESIS

GAME SESSIONS: To record and broadcast a game session you will need software that allows you to capture the images that appear on your screen. The king of free software for this type of task is undoubtedly OBS. Free, versatile, sometimes even used by professional broadcasters. Thanks to the Screen Capture or Display Capture feature, which you will locate once you open the scenes menu, you will easily be able to capture the match you are playing straight from your monitor. OBS is a comprehensive software that allows you not only to show titles and subtitles during the live broadcast but also to stream the session thanks to the built-in encoder. In addition to the game session, if you wish to broadcast your gaming station in a screen corner, as many gamers do, you will need a webcam to frame you and a microphone to pick up your voice. In this regard I would recommend light-heartedly, because I 've tested and used it, the Logitech c920 (or some of its older sisters) which is one of the most popular home webcams. As a USB microphone I would personally lean toward the Rode NT UBS. Finally, a small, inexpensive LED spotlight that lights up your face can be a great solution to improve the quality of the footage shot by the webcam. With a little well-directed light, you can hide the under-eye bags, and no one will notice that you have been up all night reading this book.

VLOG: The configuration required for a Vlog (videoblog) may be slightly different. Of course, even in this case you could scenically set up a corner of your room and use a medium-low-end webcam but, let's always remember, the audience that follows you must be well respected and if your broadcast turns out to be of dubious quality well, at first they will point it out to you then they will lose interest in your content decreeing the failure of the project. This is an especially important point both for those who are just getting into the subject and for professionals. Carefully set up your streaming, pay attention to the small details because they are the ones that will allow you to achieve a quality broadcast by standing out from the competitors. If, for example, you own and use a 4K camera, LED studio lights and a high-performance Sennheiser microphone, but a messy room lurks behind you, or you don't look presentable, your investment in professional equipment will have been completely useless.

The details, always keep them in mind.

For a quality vlog I would personally set myself up with a small green screen or a nicely arranged real background. Three small LED spotlights (two to illuminate the green screen, if present, and one for direct lighting of your figure), an entry level camera such as the Panasonic HC-V770 and a microphone that could be the Rode Wireless GO. All managed by the free OBS software. Why do I suggest the Panasonic HC-V770? It is not so much for the video quality, which with a well-lit scene will always be quite good, but for the audio quality. This Panasonic (you can also find other entry level models with the same feature) does in fact have a microphone input. In the case of live streaming, a mistake to be avoided at all costs is to send the audio and video signals via two separate channels, for example the video signal via USB input (remember that if you use an external camera other than the webcam, you will inevitably need an HDMI-to-USB capture card) and the audio signal via the microphone input, whether of the desktop or notebook. A setup where audio and video are fed into the mixing software through two separate channels will result in a desynchronisation between audio and video that will look very unprofessional. You know when the movement of your lips does not match the speech you are listening to? To avoid this issue, it is always important to capture audio and video from the same input. So, a proper external microphone plugged into the camera's audio input and the video camera itself connected to the notebook via HDMI-USB capture card. This way the audio and video signals will be synchronised and the encoding of the multimedia feed you are about to send to the cloud will also be perfectly synchronised. All directing software offers the option to solve this problem by adjusting the audio delay settings. However, there is no reason to complicate life when you can eliminate the problem at root level.

COMMERCIAL COMMUNICATIONS: if you represent a company intending to produce broadcasts for commercial purposes, it becomes important to structure your set-up with great care. The cost increases substantially, but the result is guaranteed, and with perseverance and dedication the conversions into acquired customers will confirm this. As far as cameras are concerned, the obvious choice is Pan/Tilt/Zoom, the PTZs we discussed earlier.

Their functionality as automatic tools become truly useful when it comes to a hybrid meeting, i.e., with remote guests and bystanders attending. A simple notebook connected to them via IP will allow the operator to manage the framing while going virtually unnoticed. The choice of microphone could go in the direction of a good environmental mic, which has the characteristic of being able to pick up the audio of all those present with clarity and quality. A large monitor will be essential to allow local attendees to see the guests online and be able to interact with them more naturally.

PROFESSIONAL SETUP: The devices needed to build a multi-camera setup that could be considered professional are worth hundreds of dollars. By the way, in my experience as a director of live shows, I have never had to deal with a live stream that was like something I had already done before: each new project was always unique and each client gave me, as is to be expected, new priorities and needs that forced me to adapt the set-up in a different way. Sometimes I use the hardware director or the software director only, sometimes I send the video output from vMix into the hardware director to run graphics and multimedia, or I do the exact opposite by sending the hardware director's feed into the PC, via a capture card, in order to exploit the full potential of the mixing software and let a dedicated operator mix the incoming video feeds. A professional setup must also be redundant: you should be able at any time to promptly step in with a replacement device in the case that a component does not operate as it should: it may be a cable, a converter, an adapter or any kind of interference disrupting the video feed in whatever way. Sometimes, I'll clarify for the less experienced, a control desk can include two notebooks with two software switchers, the hardware switcher, a device to record, three or four more notebooks to manage remotely connected guests, the main encoder and the backup encoder, audio mixer to mix microphones, and the commentary station (with one more audio mixer, headphones and preview monitor) in case of a sporting event.

When this happens, management software via Ip (Companion, Central Control) comes in very handy. Thanks to so-called 'macros', the operator will be able to simultaneously interact with all these different devices at the touch of a single key. Once networked together via router, these devices can be handled more easily and, above all, simultaneously. Macros are in fact preset operations that at the touch of a button trigger cascading events in fast succession on different devices. With a macro I can, at the touch of a single button, put a subtitle on air, make the camera change frame, insert a background soundtrack and initialise a recording locally, all at the same time.

Macros need to be carefully set up in advance, but once programmed, managing the live broadcast will prove much easier.

And please remember: in case you suddenly notice that a device is not working as it should, don't panic and quickly have a look at the power supply: it's unplugged.

STREAMING NETIQUETTE

In the same way as in real life, in virtual life too we must always bear in mind that the people with whom we communicate must be treated with politeness and respect. These values are not only expressed with the politeness of a 'good morning' or 'good evening', which are still fundamental. In the case of a live broadcast, politeness and respect start from the moment we are on the screen. Therefore professionalism, care for one's figure, politeness and, possibly, a pinch of sympathy. Sarcasm should be avoided: through a display, the acceptance of a witty joke may be less positive than during a face-to-face meeting. This is because behind a display, the ability to communicate with 'non-verbal' expressions (facial expressions) comes up against objective limits. Who we are, what we do and how we do it are all aspects that viewers instinctively perceive the moment we appear on their device's screen, a bit like the first glimpse of falling in love. Afterwards, it may be a good idea not to tag six hundred people every time you go live or post content. Being tagged in a way that does not concern us - I imagine you have experienced this feeling yourself - is really perceived as an unpleasant action that most of the time only wastes time, since, driven by curiosity, we will surely have a look at it to find out the reason for the tag.

Also remember that everything that happens online will stay online for a long time: even if you try to delete the memory of one of your speeches containing a blatant gaffe, someone will have already recorded it and spread it on other virtual channels before you have even finished the broadcast. It has already happened that well-established careers, even of recognised professionals, have imploded as a result of a single word said the wrong way during a live broadcast, so be careful how you express yourself especially in times like these where digitally hating seems to have become a national sport.

Finally, the quality of the broadcast. The quickest way to lose the attention of those who are watching your live show is to deliver a broadcast in which the video keeps buffering, perhaps because you are sending the feed at a bitrate that is too high, or the audio is bad because you are talking into a microphone bought at the country market. Planning and taking care of every aspect of your multimedia production is therefore the key to communicate not only the passion and commitment you put into your work but also the respect you show to those who follow you or to the client who hired you for the production.

As Sir Robert Stephenson Smyth Baden-Powell, gallant General of the British Army and founder of the Scout movement, was fond of saying: 'Try and leave this world a little better than you found it'.

This can also be done with your live broadcast.

ABOUT THE AUTHOR

Massimo Coloso was born in Cormòns in Friuli Venezia Giulia, Italy, January 6th, 1972. After graduating in classical Piano at the Trieste Conservatory, he became passionate about the digital world first as a blogger and then as a copywriter. He is a consultant for multimedia communication and owner of Mc Produzioni Video, a company that deals with technical live multicamera productions for corporate events. He currently lives in Friuli Venezia Giulia, loves walks in the hills, and enjoys the company of his beloved dogs, Leo and Tobia.

Contact the author: mcvideoinfo@gmail.com

LIVE STREAMING BASICS

EVERYTHING YOU NEED TO GET STARTED
SIMPLY EXPLAINED